JUST LIKE

LIKE

You

JUST LIKE You

Dennis A. McIntyre

PRIMIX
PUBLISHING
THE WRITE CHOICE

Primix Publishing
East Brunswick Office Evolution
1 Tower Center Boulevard, Ste 1510
East Brunswick, NJ 08816
www.primixpublishing.com
Phone: 1-800-538-5788

Published by Primix Publishing: 01/21/2026

ISBN: 979-8-89194-586-9(sc)
ISBN: 979-8-89194-587-6(e)

Library of Congress Control Number: 2025925239

CONTENTS

FOREWORD

*P*arenting is a lifelong job. At least that is what I believed until reading Malik Corey's book "In My Father's Shoes." Malik's father left as soon as he learned of the words "I'm pregnant." Malik shares that the words "You're just like your father" followed his actions, good and bad, and the effect they had on his life. He never met his father until later in life. Yet, his absence left unmistakable scars. His father was a womanizer, addict, and alcoholic, which Malik followed close behind.

Single parenting is a tough job. My heart goes out to all those dedicated people who try to raise children to be respectable and responsible adults. Children, especially young men, need their father's guidance. With a divorce rate over fifty percent, many children develop psychological, emotional and sometimes physical issues that can lead to destruction. They may have questions like, "What did I do to cause mom or dad to leave?" or "Why did dad abandon me?" They can lose trust in adult guidance, even with the best intensions. Self-doubts or faith in anything but themselves may become the normal in their lives, until they meet others going through similar experiences. A downward spiral leading to feelings of hopelessness or even worse, anger, can result.

Mass shootings in public places seems to make the headlines at an alarming rate. When the underlying causes are revealed, broken homes and the lack of parental guidance jump to the top of the list. One of my goals for writing this book is to bring awareness to fathers that their role is crucial if future generations become responsible citizens.

Malik, ultimately found and made peace with his father, but it took his heavenly father's love to reverse the negative impacts in his life. He went from a womanizer to a devote husband by the grace of God. He pioneered and became CEO of a foundation to help others conquer their internal demons.

Whether you are young, approaching retirement years or older, consider this question:

If I were able to observe my eulogy, what would I hope people say?

Then consider the life you ar e living and examine if that measures up. You may consider yourself as a complete success with all that you accomplished. Then, you would expect the words to reflect elements of those good works. How would you react if a son or daughter used words like, "Dad was never around" or "I wish that I spent more time with him." Words like these can cut to our heart. Our children may feel a separation caused by the drive to succeed.

Now consider the father who made family such a high

priority that promotions were turned down when they meant leaving them. Words like "He rarely missed my ball game" or "I knew he loved me." might be uttered in his passing.

Finally, consider your son or daughter sharing their heartfelt words of affirmation why you are alive. That happened to me. This is my story.

"THAT'S JUST LIKE YOU, DAD."

*M*any of us can recall precious moments in our lives when those we cherish provide words or deeds that reach deep down into our souls. A wellspring of tremendous joy and affirmation flows. These were the words from my son that had such an effect.

The year was 2000. My father was in a nursing home after having a stroke two years earlier. I took an early retirement from upstate New York and spent the last fourteen months ministering to dad on the weekends. That meant that I had to leave my wife but felt God's calling. We were empty nesters and the thought of my father alone in the nursing home tugged at my heart. A friend offered a position with his firm in Orlando about forty-five minutes west of Merritt Island where the nursing home was located. That covered my living expenses while my wife stayed in our home in upstate New York. Dad was getting much weaker and that day meant delivering fast food for us to enjoy in his room. My son called my cell phone as I entered the facility.

Dad: "Hello."

Son: "Hi dad. Just thought I'd call."

Dad: "Great to hear from you. What's up?"

Son: "All is well. How about you?"

Dad: "Just stopped for burgers and fries by the   nursing home. Hang on a minute."

I paused to place the order and then continued the conversation. A second pause came when I reached the register to pay for the order. Conversation resumed as I held the phone by my ear with a bag of food in my left hand. As I pushed the door open with my foot, a man stared me in the face.

"Could you spare some food, mister?"

The bag was placed in his hand, and I returned to reorder. Somehow, I was able to maintain my conversation with my son as I reentered the restaurant.

"What was that all about, dad?"

I explained about the man asking for a meal and that I was placing a new food order. Then the defining moment came forever etched in my heart and mind.

"Oh dad. That's just like you."

Fatherhood was extremely important to me. I lost my mother to cancer when I was three. The next five years were spent with my two brothers in various foster homes while dad tried to get his life back together. Mom was the bread winner, so everything was lost in her passing. Dad dropped out of school when his father died to help his mother. After four years in heavy WWII battles, he returned home to start a new life with the one who was there in spirit with him in the trenches. Three sons were born between 1946 and 1949. The terrors of war were replaced with the joy of starting a family.

Mom was of Jewish descent but embraced Christianity and accepted Christ before her death. I can only imagine dad's anguish, but I know that keeping his three boys together was foremost on his heart. He remarried five years later, and we became a family again. Although we lived meagerly by world standards, we were rich.

Those five years away from my father left a void that would not be filled until I had a family of my own. I attended church with my wife, but fatherhood left me with some doubts. I accepted Christ before the birth of my daughter and pleaded with God for guidance as a father. I desired to provide for my family in every way but needed help when it came to fatherhood. My math and science skills could be a great help when they entered their high school years, but far above their skillset when they were infants. That was my wife's role while I repaired broken toys or playfully wrestled them on the living room floor. Parenting was a team event. I was fifty-three when my son's words came. He was thirty and married with a family of his own. Those words were heartfelt and powerful. It was God's "well done" affirmation to me.

I tried to teach him many things over the years. He observed me working with my hands, but those skills were not successfully passed down. Still, the thought that I would help someone in need in a moment left an impression. "Oh dad. That's just like you." He said that while living in Texas, a thousand miles away. Yet, it was as if he was right there witnessing the act. He pictured my response in his mind as if there was no doubt. The man asked for food and without hesitation, I gave it to him. It was a defining moment for me that I had succeeded as a father.

I also thanked God for bringing me to that place at that time. The many weekends spent with dad, ultimately, led to his salvation. That was another defining moment in my life. Dad had turned away from God and seemed to blame Him for taking his wife. On October 1, 2000, I told my father that I had to leave early. My pastor asked me if I had ever been baptized. I told him "No." Then I said that I would like to do that publicly. Three o'clock that afternoon was the scheduled time. Baptism may have been something that my mother desired or went through before her death, as dad's heart was stirred. I lead him in three prayers while sitting in the front seat of my van. Three weeks later, I asked for confirmation that my eighty-nine-year-old father knew what he prayed. God provided an exclamation mark.

My life was planned before I was born. My early childhood left me screaming "Doesn't anybody love me" after some rough moments in foster care. As a father I learned that God was with me all the time. The love of a godly wife and concern for others in need shaped my character as confirmed by my son. Later, during my wife's battle with cancer, I read Ephesians 2 verse 10.

> *For we are God's handiwork, created in Christ Jesus*
> *to do good works, which God prepared in advance*
> *for us to do.*

God is faithful. Events in life may appear as roadblocks but God sees the bigger picture. He is not constrained by time like we are. There are no accidents with Him. The scales of bitterness fell from my father's eyes that day in the van and God took him home before turning ninety. The nursing home left somber thoughts in my mind. Knowing that dad is with Jesus replaced those thoughts with utter joy.

After his conversion, I asked dad who he would see in heaven. Without hesitation, he responded, "Your mother." Three weeks later, my older brother made the three-hour trip from South Florida to be with dad. He took him out of the home to observe the catch on the pier. On the ride back, dad started singing. Two words were long sentences to our father. We never heard him sing before, so the scene was strange. What was stranger was that he was singing "When the Roll is Called Up Yonder," an old hymn from his childhood. He had come full circle and confirmed my prayer that he was in God's care.

I remember trying to pass on math skills to my son when he entered high school. He was failing at the time as indicated by his test scores and lack of acceptable homework. Soon afterwards, he started getting all the right answers on his homework. I felt good until those papers were graded by his teacher with low scores. He fully understood the assigned problems, but I failed to lead him with a step-by-step methodology. Later, I was taking a night school calculus course at a local college and was downgraded for not showing all my work. I got the right answers, but the instructor wanted more. It wasn't until I approached the teacher after class that I got resolution. He put a problem on the board and before he wrote "Find F/x," I wrote the answer on the board. I may have had the right intensions on helping my son in math, but that was not enough. He needed other support.

Fathers protect, guide, nurture, instruct and apply

consequences as needed for wrong behavior. These were foreign concepts to Malik as he recalled the first thirty years of his life. His actions mimicked the father he never knew without consequences until his actions brought him before a judge who sentenced him to jail. He is not alone in society today. Many young men find their leadership in a bottle, drugs or a gang. Oh, how they need a father's love.

"Oh dad. That's just like you."

I may not have used the right skills to teach my son algebra due to my own limitations, but the time spent was not in vain. He understood what I shared and needed others to complete the learning process. That is what life teaches us every day. Only one source has all the answers. Over the years I witnessed lives changed through spoken words that could only have come from God, who has been leading me.

I was reminded of a story that I heard about a young schoolboy running to catch a train with an armload of books. A man ran past him knocking the books from the boy's hands. Then he realized what he did, let the train pass and turned to help gather the books. After they were resecured in the child's arms, he started to leave. The boy called to him and said these words.

"Mister. Be you Jesus?"

Imagine the reaction as the man turned around. He caused the dilemma. Yet, those words were far more than a "thank you." He may have told the boy that he was sorry. He certainly did not feel that he earned such favor, but to that child he was Jesus. Someone must have taught the boy about who Jesus is and what He did. All the boy knew was Jesus helped people. Missing the train that day was not an accident, nor was the words from my son.

Questions to ponder:

1. What does my legacy look like?

2. What role model do I demonstrate to my children?

3. How would I respond to my father's actions?

4. Am I acting like my father?

5. Do I need a change in direction?

THE GARDEN

Let's take a step back and examine fatherhood. The book of Genesis begins with God's blueprint for creation. The first five days of creation provides a lush garden with animals, sunshine, and water. God said it was "Good." On the sixth day man was created and God said it was "Very good." Man was separated from the rest of the creation as he was made in "God's image." Later we read that man was formed out of the dust and was brought to life by His breath. Genesis 2:7 tells us that man became a "Living being" or in other versions a "Living soul."

God was the father and began establishing specific instructions for how man was to live. Like an earthly father, God provided everything to support life. The garden would provide an abundance of food with one exception. Man was not to eat from the "Tree of the Knowledge of Good and Evil." (Genesis 2:17) That may seem like a simple instruction but it implied that man had a choice. God desired an intimate relationship with his creation and chose man. Free will was a risky gift but necessary for intimacy.

We might surmise that Adam walked and talked with the Father in the garden for a season. He may have shunned away from the Tree of the Knowledge of Good and Evil in obedience. At some point God desired an earthly helpmate for Adam. The intimacy that He enjoyed was a gift for Adam to share. Adam was put to sleep, a rib was removed and a helpmate was created. The concept of marriage between a man and a woman was revealed. Adam's rib became a symbol where "Two will become One (Genesis 2:24)." Then things changed.

We don't read that Adam passed on to his bride, Eve, God's command to not eat of one tree. We know that he did, based on the serpent's words in Genesis 3:1-3:

> [1]*Now the serpent was more crafty than any of the wild animals the Lord God had made. He said to the woman, "Did God really say, 'You must not eat from any tree in the garden'?"*

> [2] *The woman said to the serpent, "We may eat fruit from the trees in the garden,*

> [3] *but God did say, 'You must not eat fruit from the tree that is in the middle of the garden, and you must not touch it, or you will die.'"*

Satan was a rebellious angel fallen from God's grace. Suddenly, he appears as a serpent in the garden. He was aware of everything God shared with creation. Pride consumed him and he desired to be on an equal plane with God. The concept of death should have been foreign to Eve. She may have uttered those words, but they may have appeared odd. Then we read Genesis 3:4-7:

> [4]*"You will not certainly die," the serpent said to the woman.*
>
> [5] *"For God knows that when you eat from it your eyes will be opened, and you will be like God, knowing good and evil."*
>
> [6] *When the woman saw that the fruit of the tree was good for food and pleasing to the eye, and also desirable for gaining wisdom, she took some and ate it. She also gave some to her husband, who was with her, and he ate it.*
>
> [7] *Then the eyes of both of them were opened, and they realized they were naked; so they sewed fig leaves together and made coverings for themselves.*

Satan used a half-truth to lure Eve into choosing to eat from the tree. Good and evil would become known to her. After giving the fruit to Adam, both their eyes were opened. They realized they were naked. They knew that they disobeyed the Father and God allowed them to feel guilt and separation from Him. They tried to hide from God. Then they tried to focus the blame away from themselves. Penalties for disobedience were issued by God. Adam would have to work for food. Eve would have pain in childbirth. Satan would ultimately be defeated.

The concept of fatherhood was initiated soon afterwards.

Chapter four begins with the birth of two sons, Cain and then Abel. Cain was given the responsibility to work the soil, while Abel tended the flocks of animals. God desired offerings from them both. Cain offered products from his fields. Abel offered "Fatted first-born animals." Nothing of description defined Cain's offering, while Abel's showed reverence and respect with the words "fatted" and "first-born." Abel's offering was acceptable to God, indicating respect and thoughtfulness. Cain's offering did not have the same affect. Cain responded to God's acceptance of his brother's gift with his anger by killing Abel.

Society seems to give first-born children special privileges and added responsibilities. Birthrights were upheld in Jewish law for inheritances. Cain felt that he deserved more. Jealousy and pride reared their ugly heads as he struck his brother down in the field. Like Adam (his father) Cain tried to cover his offense. God told him that his brother's blood cries out from the ground. Cain was punished as the land would no longer yield good crops, and he would become a wanderer. He felt the punishment was too harsh. Then he feared for his life. God placed a mark on him to keep others from killing him. He headed east away from his family.

We are not told about other inhabitants that he would encounter. But chapter five tells us that he found a wife, and she bore children. The first (vs.17) was given the name "Enoch." Verse 24 informs us the "Enoch walked with God." Cain must have passed on the things of God and assumed his role as a father. God showed His mercy.

Questions to ponder:

1. Do you believe Darwin's theory that we are inhabitants by chance?

2. If you believe that you have been placed here for a reason, then have you discovered what that looks like?

3. Do you believe that without help, undesired behaviors can affect future generations?

4. Do you know your mission?

SINS OF THE FATHER

The sin of abandonment is one that refuses to take ownership and responsibility. In many ways it leaves its mark with the child wondering "What's wrong with me?" That alone leaves emotional scars that may last a lifetime. Children feel unloved and unworthy of being loved. They reach out for acceptance, often through the wrong crowds. Since their mother was also abandoned, respect for women is severely diminished. Malik took on these same characteristics in his adult life. Words like "You're just like your father" or "You have your father's ___" are uttered without the child ever knowing their father.

Adam disobeyed God and partook of the fruit. He didn't respect God's command. Cain must have known that God desired the best offering. Otherwise, why would God' be upset with it. Sin has a way of passing from generation to generation. In Genesis chapter 12, Abram lies to Pharoah. Sarah was beautiful and he thought his life was in danger if he said she was his wife. So, he referred to Sarah as his sister. Genesis 12: 10-20:

> [10] *Now there was a famine in the land, and Abram went down to Egypt to live there for a while because the famine was severe.* [11] *As he was about to enter Egypt, he said to his wife Sarai, "I know what a beautiful woman you are.* [12] *When the Egyptians see you, they will say, 'This is his wife.' Then they will kill me but will let you live.* [13] *Say you are my sister, so that I will be treated well for your sake and my life will be spared because of you."*

> [14] *When Abram came to Egypt, the Egyptians saw that Sarai was a very beautiful woman.* [15] *And when Pharaoh's officials saw her, they praised her to Pharaoh, and she was taken into his palace.* [16] *He treated Abram well for her sake, and Abram acquired sheep and cattle, male and female donkeys, male and female servants, and camels.*

> [17] *But the Lord inflicted serious diseases on Pharaoh and his household because of Abram's wife Sarai.* [18] *So Pharaoh summoned Abram. "What have you done to   me?" he said. "Why didn't you tell me she was your wife?* [19] *Why did you say, 'She is my sister,' so that I took her to be my wife? Now then, here is your wife. Take her and go!"* [20] *Then Pharaoh gave orders about Abram to his men, and they sent him on his way, with his wife and everything he had.*

It is interesting that Pharoah's response was one of fear. He gave wealth to Abram. Then God inflicted serious diseases on Pharoah creating fear in his heart. Then we read Genesis 26: 1-11:

> *¹Now there was a famine in the land—besides the previous famine in Abraham's time—and Isaac went to Abimelek king of the Philistines in Gerar. ² The Lord appeared to Isaac and said, "Do not go down to Egypt; live in the land where I tell you to live. ³ Stay in this land for a while, and I will be with you and will bless you. For to you and your descendants I will give all these lands and will confirm the oath I swore to your father Abraham. ⁴ I will make your descendants as numerous as the stars in the sky and will give them all these lands, and through your offspring all nations on earth will be blessed, ⁵ because Abraham obeyed me and did everything I required of him, keeping my commands, my decrees and my instructions." ⁶ So Isaac stayed in Gerar. ⁷ When the men of that place asked him about his wife, he said, "She is my sister," because he was afraid to say, "She is my wife." He thought, "The men of this place might kill me on account of Rebekah, because she is beautiful."*

> *⁸ When Isaac had been there a long time, Abimelek king of the Philistines looked down from a window and saw Isaac caressing his wife Rebekah. ⁹ So Abimelek summoned Isaac and said, "She is really your wife! Why did you say, 'She is my sister'?"*

Isaac answered him, "Because I thought I might lose my life on account of her."

[10] Then Abimelek said, "What is this you have done to us? One of the men might well have slept with your wife, and you would have brought guilt upon us."

[11] So Abimelek gave orders to all the people: "Anyone who harms this man or his wife shall surely be put to death."

Isaac was not born when Abram lied. Later, God changed Abram's name to Abraham and made a covenant with him as the father of many nations. That promise was passed on to Isaac. Yet, we see the same sin committed by Isaac for the same reason. Sin entered the life of the father and was passed down to the son.

Some sins are learned by observation. We watch our father smoke or drink alcohol. Then we repeat the same habits. Until something reverses the cycle, generations to follow are also infected. The father's role becomes crucial to continuing the trend or ending it.

Questions to ponder:

1. Why do you think the Bible records human history?

2. Do you believe that history repeats itself?

3. Are there areas of life that you wish would change for the better?

4. Are you willing to be an advocate for positive change?

STICKS AND STONES

We have all heard the words "Sticks and stones can break your bones but names will never hurt you." Those words are so far from the truth. The words we say can be uplifting or detrimental. I remember a close friend's conversation one day, that involved a little league baseball game where his father attended. My friend's name was Eric. After striking out three times in the game, his father greeted him with the words "Come on strike out king. Let's get some ice cream." On the surface those words may sound good. After all, they came with a treat. Eric shared that they could not have been more hurtful. They stayed with him well into adulthood and severely challenged his self-worth. His marriage was in trouble and counselling was an attempt for reconciliation.

The Psychologist uncovered those harmful words and knew Eric's lack of self-esteem stemmed from them. Eric was handed a pillow and told that it represented his father who had passed away. The moment of truth was at hand. He could not get resolution directly with his father, so the pillow was used as substitute. After further instruction, Eric began beating the pillow with intensity. Anger had welled up inside him for all those years and was now released. As Eric shared that story with me, I could see many emotions. The last one came with tears in his eyes. He truly loved his father, but those words filled his heart with pain. He also shared that was the last time he played baseball.

Sometimes the things we say, that are meant to encourage, can have the opposite effect. I remember the time when my grandmother passed away. I was working as an electrician in a large company. My boss sent me to support another supervisor for the week. I requested time off for the funeral from the new boss and it was granted without hesitation. He told me to take the whole day off. As I was leaving, I passed my boss' office and as a curtesy stopped in to share that I would not be in the next day. He may have thought that his words were meant to encourage me as to my value to his organization, but they had the opposite effect. Rather than tell me that all was well, he said words like "Oh! I really could use you ..." I felt anger as I was not assigned to him that week. Looking back, I could see that he was trying to let me know how valuable I was to him, but his words came at the wrong time.

Words can affirm us. On another occasion I was assigned to a delicate job in a lab with volatile chemicals just prior to the Christmas holidays. The lab technicians needed electrical work done so they could work over the holidays when everyone else was off. When I returned to work, I was called into the department head's office. I was apprehensive as all I could think about was the work that I did in the lab. Negative thoughts permeated my mind. When I walked into the office, I heard the words "Remember the job you did before the holidays in the lab." My heart sunk. All I could think about was that a catastrophe occurred. Those chemicals may have exploded or caught fire. My self-talk went down a dark path. After nodding in agreement, he continued, "I just received a call from the lead chemist." Once again, my heart lumped in my throat. Then the words "Well done" was followed by the affirmation that the tests went flawlessly.

The apprehension of being called into the top manager's office was quickly relieved. Many of us go through similar feelings when the flashing lights of a police car tell us to pull over. Negative thoughts enter our consciousness until the officer wants to alert us to a danger ahead or that a taillight is not working. Words are powerful.

Consider the words of Jesus on the cross when His time was near and the Roman soldiers were casting lots for His clothes below. Luke 23: 34 says: *"Father, forgive them, for they do not know what they are doing."* Jesus hung in agony as an innocent man and yet forgave His accusers. Perhaps, the Roman soldiers may have thought He was talking to them as they cast lots. In any case they were not words of accusation but of love. Those words were recorded and etched in humanity for eternity.

Consider your response to hearing words like "You're just like your father." Malik never knew his father. So, how could he understand what those words meant? Others may know their father all their lives and still wonder how to interpret them. Their father may have been loving at times or angry at other times. We would try and reflect on what just happened to cause those words to be uttered. Were they meant to mimic positive traits or something less desirable? Depending how they are interpreted can make all the difference to a person's psyche. Like Eric, his father's words may have been meant to make light of the situation but caused deep internal pain. Sticks and stones can hurt but so can our words.

The Jewish leaders observed Jesus healing a demon-possessed man recorded in Mathew 12:22-24:

> *22 Then they brought him a demon-possessed man who was blind and mute, and Jesus healed him, so that he could both talk and see. 23 All the people were astonished and said, "Could this be the Son of David?"*

> *24 But when the Pharisees heard this, they said, "It is only by Beelzebul, the prince of demons, that this fellow drives out demons."*

After Jesus defended Himself, he focused on the Pharisees motives. In Matthew 12:34 we read these words:

> *34 You brood of vipers, how can you who are evil say anything good? For the mouth speaks what the heart is full of.*

Talk about words that pierce, those leaders received a dagger. Our lives before Christ can store unwholesome talk that can quickly flow out our mouths. Consider a time when you accidently hit your thump with a hammer. What came out of your mouth? I can imagine that it was far from uplifting. Calling those leaders a "brood of vipers" was not meant to encourage their behavior. Out of the heart the mouth speaks. The hearts of the Pharisees were prideful. Their words reflected their pride.

Jesus desires to dwell in our heart. If we let Him guide from our heart, powerful things can happen. Many of the words that have left my mouth did not come from my mind. Often, I did not know why I said them until later. In my "Coffee Shop Ministries" book I shared a story titled "The Flight." At the last minute I decided to fly down to Florida to visit my parents. I arrived at the airport and tried to get a seat assignment. I found out that the flight was overbooked. I was offered a free ticket and a seat on the next flight. The first-class ticket holders boarded first. Then, after a half hour delay, the remaining passengers boarded. Another half hour passed, and I was called up to get my next flight assignment. To my surprise I was told that the flight had not left. One seat was available in first-class. As quickly as I boarded, the plane began to taxi.

An elderly lady was sitting in my row by the window. Initially, I tried to start a conversation, but she seemed to not want to share. The stewardesses tried to offer refreshments, a blanket or a pillow without response. Once the plane became air born, I was able to introduce myself. I learned that she came to New York by car with her husband and that he passed away suddenly. The car was left with their daughter, and she was heading home to make funeral arrangements. Then she asked me why I was going to Florida. After telling her about my parents, words came out of my mouth that could have only come from the Holy Spirit. I said, "I wish I could do more."

After sharing that I wished I could help them financially with a newer car, she came out of her shell with words like:

"YOUNG MAN! They don't care about your money or gifts. They just want to know that you care. Going down to see them is more than enough."

I felt like I had been reprimanded. The rest of the flight was a pleasure as we both shared memories together. I don't remember thinking that I wished I could do more, but God knew those were the words that she needed to hear. As we were about to start the decent, she got up to use the facilities. Three stewardesses came to me with joy on their faces. They each hugged me and thanked me. For an hour before take-off, they tried everything to improve her demeanor without success. Watching her perk up, as she did, touched their hearts. I am no longer amazed when the right words come out that cause hearts to stir.

Questions to ponder:

1. Have you been hurt by something others said?

2. How did the words make you feel?

3. What did you do about it?

4. Have you had an experience where something you said change someone's life (good or bad)?

5. Have you ever felt that the words you said came outside of yourself?

ACTIONS SPEAK VOLUMES

"Oh dad. That's just like you." The response from my son came after something that I did. He wasn't there to witness the event, but he had seen me respond in a similar manner over the years. My reaction to the man requesting food was without hesitation. Children learn from observing their parents. Sons tend to gravitate towards their fathers, while daughters watch their moms. A son may not have a desire to learn how to cook like their mother, although that's not always the case. Dad may teach him how to throw a baseball or catch a fish. Putting a worm on a hook may seem gross to a girl but not to a boy. I remember a country song with the words "Watching you, dad. Ain't it cool." In the lyrics the father observes his son uttering a profane word or praying. What a testimony about how our actions affect the growth of our children.

Single parent homes have been rising in America over the past decades. Affluence, the Internet, and other conditions may be the cause. People are being taught to be anything they desire. Media has become the parental guide for so many young people. Family time has changed from eating regular meals at home to facetime on a cell phone. Young people gravitate towards the actions of friends and idols. The words "Til death do us part" are replaced by "If it doesn't work out, I'll find someone else." This scenario has greatly diminished a value system from the past, where long term commitments were the norm.

Boys need a father figure in their lives. If dad is not there, they will find someone or something to replace him. They need to know they have worth and may find it in a street gang or a corner bar. A father is the biggest role model in a son's life. Yet, many fathers fail to understand their roles. Malik's father bolted from his life as soon as he learned that his son was about to be born. He had no desire to nurture him. Responsibility was only limited to caring for himself. Even with his father's lack of presence in his life, Malik was told many times while growing up that he was "just like his father." How can that be? He never knew him and yet he was just like him. There is something in the human gene pool that instills common traits beyond appearance.

In 2010 I was introduced to a Florida man whose father abandoned him when he was four years old. A friend invited me to record the man's life and write his story. The result was my book titled, "Shackled Yet Free." The early years were in direct contrast to the man that I was interviewing. Drugs, alcohol, gangs, and jail were part of his downward spiral until a judge saw something worth saving in him. The judge introduced him to his heavenly father, and a new set of values shaped his life. The rage inside began to be replaced with love. Abandonment is a powerful force to anyone, especially a young boy. It screams words like "Doesn't daddy love me?" or "Am I the reason daddy left?" Questions like these are often unanswered and simmer like hot coals in a child's heart. Love cannot be felt.

Contrast this scene with the father who does not leave and demonstrates love daily. The child knows that their questions will be answered. A father's smile brightens their day. Laughter becomes infectious. The child becomes an adult able to laugh and love in their future relationships. The action of their father speaks volumes.

Consider Noah and his family in Genesis chapter nine. They worked together building an ark, even when a flood was unheard of. Three young men followed their father's instructions when it may have made no sense. They ate together, prayed together and perhaps, laughed together. After the flood subsided, they began a new life together, until Ham found his father drunk from the wine of the vineyard. Noah's response sent Ham and his family away. No longer would a father's love be there for Ham to enjoy. Ham's journey takes him through places like Sodom, Gomorrah, Nineveh, and Babel. Negative cultures became Ham's new teachers. The Bible does not let us know that Noah made peace with his son before his death. Ham was abandoned and the effect was not a good one.

My father returned from WWII as a decorated veteran. He wanted to put the terror of war behind him as he returned home. Holding the woman who kept him sane in the trenches and starting a family was foremost on his heart. They married and in less than three years three sons were born. I was the middle child. Thoughts of the war were replaced with spending quality time with his boys. Mom was the bread winner, so dad was the caretaker. Love, joy and laughter abounded. Then tragedy struck. Cancer took a wife and mother from the scene, leaving a father in debt, without a job, and three boys to care for, all under the age of five.

Despite the enormous obstacles to overcome, dad persevered. He was determined to keep his sons together while he sought employment. He tried to get family members to help, but that was short-lived. An acquaintance offered to care for his boys along with her daughter, which dad could not refuse. After various unsatisfactory conditions occurred, dad was forced to seek foster care. He landed a minimum wage job and rented a room close by. He did not own a car, so visitation with his sons was limited. More negative feedback from the foster home led him to find a new one. A farmer and his wife took the boys in. It was the first and last place where love was felt until dad remarried. During their dating he was able to visit his sons, because she had a car. We looked forward to those weekends when we knew dad was coming.

Early in our time spent on the farm, the farmer approached my older brother with words like:

"You don't have a mother, so you can call my wife mom. You have a father so call me grandpa."

Those words had a profound effect on my older brother. A bond was created that would later bring about rebellion. After five years of foster care, we became a family again. The mother that I never knew became real for me. I missed the love and affection of a father during those years and looked forward to rebuilding new relationships. The idea of a third mother was difficult for my older brother to accept. He was the only child that remembered our mom. When the farmer's wife became "mom," he felt the love and affection all over again. One day he jumped on his Schwinn bicycle and pedaled about twenty miles back to the farm. When he arrived, he learned that "mom" was near death. The farmer called our father, let him know that his son was okay, and that he would bring him back the next day. Dad must have understood and did not offer repercussions. That event offered closure for my brother.

While living on the farm, we were bussed to school, where we excelled. Now we entered the third, fourth and fifth grades at a school close to our new home. Once again, we excelled. We desired to please our mother and father in everything we did. As we entered the teenage years, we moved to a larger residence located in farm country. The high school was a two and a half mile walk but closer to where dad worked. On some occasions, he would drop us off early in his car, especially when bad weather impeded walking.

Earlier, I stated that I was the middle child. Three boys took on separate characteristics common to their birth order. My older brother (big brother) had the first-born trait. He had to learn responsibility early and applied himself academically. Straight A's, National Honor Society and full college tuition resulted.

My younger brother also earned a full scholarship and attended college shortly after graduating high school. The Viet Nam War was ongoing along with the draft. College was a viable alternative.

Although, my grades were high, I desired to work. The local farmers kept me busy all through high school. In addition, I raked leaves, shoveled snow, mowed lawns and helped dad around the yard. I filled my school curriculum with as many math courses as I could, as homework was completed before I came home. I knew that dad did not have the financial means to help me obtain the things that I desired. I saved money to purchase a car and then passed my driver's test with it a week later. After graduation, I went to work for a industrial giant until my draft number was eminent. I decided to take the Air Force tests to see where I could find a fit. The scores allowed for me to choose any career path. I chose electronics and became an autopilot technician. I worked on B52's and refueling 135 tankers.

I remember many times when I spent time alone with dad. When he worked in the garden, I was drawn to help. I recalled a time when he was on his knees placing flat stones in cement between the house and the unattached garage. I watched and assisted. Dad was a champion horseshoe pitcher. He won state tournaments and built a pit on the side of the yard for practice. I watched him throw and learned a technique of my own. He would spot me fifteen points in a game where twenty-one won. I only remember beating him one time. Once, I tossed five consecutive ringers only to watch him throw six. I observed him playing the card game of bridge, where he was a sought-after life master (highest honor). I could hold my own as his partner, which was an accomplishment as he did not enjoy those who played poorly.

I was my father's child in so many ways. The things he enjoyed, I enjoyed. Vacations were always spent fishing, usually in the Thousand Islands near the northern border of upstate New York. Dad seemed to spend more time untangling lines as he did fishing during our early years as a family. Yet, those times were special to him. When we became adults, he would entice us with a wager of a quarter for the biggest fish caught. He was never too proud to collect our quarters and claim bragging rights. Of course, we loved to win as well.

One thing that was missing in dad's life was faith. After mom died, dad seemed to blame God. He filled his life with things like bridge playing, stamp collecting, jigsaw puzzles, crosswords, books (especially westerns) and more. He did not attend church but didn't keep us from visiting. Even with a meager income, he provided for our needs. He was faithful and devoted to his family. His word was his bond. These were qualities that spoke volumes. "Oh, dad. That's just like you" reminded me of all that I learned from my father.

Questions to ponder:

1. What do you remember about your father?

2. How did his actions affect you?

3. What is your son learning by your actions?

4. What do you wish you had done differently?

HALF TIME

*I*remember reading a short book titled "Half Time" by Bob Bufford. Its premise was that men tend to begin their lives working to support their family. The work may be rewarding, but often not what gives personal satisfaction or pleasure. Men begin to take up other interests like woodworking, playing golf or even writing. For those who fail to create such an interest, forced retirement could lead to very short and unfulfilling retirements. Someone once said the definition of success is finding something you love and then finding someone to pay you to do it. I love to play golf. I am also envious of those on the senior tour who get paid to play.

Reflecting on my life and career shows me that Bob's insights held truth. I didn't start playing golf during those years when my focus was on raising a family. I corelated my Air Force training into a three-year electrical apprentice program and became an electrician. With the support of the GI bill and overtime, I secured a home and elevated myself into the electrical engineering field. My wife was also the financial manager in the family. Somehow, we were able to provide most of the college costs for our children that covered nine years. Driving the same vehicle during those years was endured, despite the salt-caused rust from the severe winters.

After the children married, my wife and I needed to create a new focus. Half-time had come. We were able to have more time to get away, visit friends, upgrade our cars and more. The idea of retirement began to surface, which was not an option while the children were home. Company retirement packages were being offered to reduce staffing due to increased pressure from competitors. Under normal conditions, retirement was something to consider when you neared sixty-two, when Social Security became available. I was fifty. Counting four years of military and twenty-eight years of work, the company credited me with thirty-two years of service. Years of service and age added together was the benchmark. Eighty-five total was considered full retirement, which. equated to about forty percent of your income. Retirement packages were offered with that number reduced to seventy-five and included two-weeks' pay for every year up to twenty-six. For me, that meant a year's pay.

The company investment program would provide added income as well. I knew that my skills as an electrical engineer would provide work and a year's salary meant that I would not need to tap any other income source for at least a year. I took the offer and the severance as half pay for two years. I started my own controls business which quickly grew. We became debt free and could see many years before Social Security would set it.

God had other plans. Dad had a stroke. He was living alone

in an apartment. When he missed a bridge date, his playing partner became alarmed. Missing the second one two days later led to contacting his building superintendent to unlock his door. They found him unconscious but alive. His head had been bleeding after striking a nightstand. They rushed him to emergency, where everything in his life dramatically changed. Like a child, he had to learn how to eat. His left side was weak. He could not read or perform simple tasks. After weeks of therapy, he was sent to a nursing home. God called me to care for him. I struggled at first but finally packed my two-door Honda accord, left my wife and made the trip to Florida.

Leaving my wife was difficult. I did not know how long I would be away, but the half-pay for two-years was ample to support her, while we awaited the birth of a grandchild. I paid off her car, so only the basic needs were left. I started working for a friend in Orlando after securing a one-bedroom apartment with only the simplest needs, like a bed, couch, and TV. Weekends were spent with my father. The two-door Accord was a challenge as I had to place his wheelchair in the open trunk tied with bungee cords. Dad's weak left side caused me to lift and place him down into the front seat. Yet, that was necessary if I was going to take him out of that awful home.

God was in control. I had the thought that I should consider looking for a used van. That would make life easier when it came to getting dad out of that place. The following Monday, I received a call at my workplace.

"Hello."

"Can you talk?"

"Yes! Who is this?"

"My name is John (alias). I have been charged with finding someone to represent my company in Florida and your name came highly regarded."

His company was a supplier of electronic controls. I had used many of his competitor's controls over the years but was not familiar with his systems. I shared that fact, but he insisted that the company would provide the necessary training. He discussed salary and asked what it would take to bring me on board. I gave him my final electrical engineering salary. He had no problem meeting it. That was about forty percent higher than I was earning. Then he hit me with these words:

"The position required a company vehicle. We usually provide a full-size car, but would you prefer a van?"

That was a WOW moment. God heard my prayer as just a thought the day before for a used van. Now I am being offered a new one, higher pay and all expenses. I thought that I was being rewarded for obeying His call. I was concerned that if I accepted the offer, my boss would feel the loss. I agreed to meet John along with a salesman at the Orlando airport later. That would give me the time to approach my boss. Not only did he give me his blessing, but he shared that it was an answer to his dilemma. The company that I supported for him had demanded that he take on a multi-million-dollar inventory. Sales was good but not high enough to support that investment. On the flip side, he did not want to fire me by telling them no. I made the airport meeting and accepted the offer.

The salesman that I reported to resided in a suburb of Orlando, called Oviedo. Within a few months, I was able to secure a two-year old three bedroom, two bath home in that town. That became another amazing moment as my wife could now have a place to stay during her visits, along with a car to drive in the driveway while I may have been away in the company van. Her best friend was only a three-hour drive south, so she could spend extended time with her. Since I travelled the whole state of Florida, many trips were planned combining business with pleasure. It was my second half career. Unlike the "Half Time" book, where we determine what that would consist of, God chose it for me.

If I modified Bob's book, I would change the title to "Quarter Time." I agreed with his concepts, but a single change in vocation is rarely the case. Working for one company for a full career is rare. That may have been true for life after WWII when large companies were growing without competition, but the fast-paced changes of the twenty-first century would hinder long term employment. Occupational interruptions are now the normal. Usually, new opportunities remain along the same avenues as previous jobs, but that was not the case for me.

After Fourteen months with my father, another milestone occurred. While sitting in the front seat of that van, I led my father in several prayers. He accepted Jesus as his Savior and my heart soared. Again, I thanked my Lord for using me. I am not sure whether it was the gift of encouragement or something else that opened Dad's heart. All I knew was that I felt God's wee voice calling me to go there and He did the rest. Dad was eighty-nine and died before reaching his ninetieth birthday.

That led to a new decision. Should I continue to work or retire? My wife insisted that I was too young to finally retire.

I think she enjoyed travelling down to Florida, especially in the wintertime. Still, I longed to be with her on a permanent basis. I enjoyed my work, but weekends were lonely. God was still in control.

Questions to ponder:

1. What does retirement look like to you?

2. How many times has your career path changed?

3. Are you satisfied with your life?

4. Do you feel that you are following your designed purpose?

FINDING OUR PURPOSE

At some point in our life, we come to ask ourselves "What is my purpose?" For some this question comes early in adulthood and they are fortunate to pursue fulfilling career paths. These people receive their answer from a higher calling, a special event, a dream or person. They feel motivated to follow through every avenue that allows them to use gifts and talents that serve their purpose. Life seems to have meaning. They look forward to all they can accomplish.

Others, like most of us, ask the question much later in life. We look back at what we have accomplished and wonder what it all means. We are unable to answer the question logically. Usually, we make feeble attempts that are far removed from what others see in us as our purpose. For example, I have a pastor friend that desired for me to be on every committee meeting that he chaired because he saw the gift of encouragement in me. When he shared that with me, I denied that it was true. I spent much of my childhood years in foster care without parental guidance. If anyone need encouragement, I felt that I should be the one receiving it. I did not believe that was a gift that I had to be used to help others.

The realization that I actually had the gift came after retiring from my first job. I had been living in an all-electric home that created a potential dilemma. The hot water heater did not reheat fast enough for everyone in the house to take morning showers which we all enjoyed. I made it a habit to shower an hour earlier than I needed so that my wife and two children could have plenty of hot water. I left the house and stopped at a local coffee house five minutes from work. People would come and go every ten or fifteen minutes while I was there for at least an hour. The habit continued even after we became empty nesters. The owner of the coffee house found out that I was leaving soon to minister to my father in Florida. As a result, she asked what day would be my last at her shop. I told her the day would be the following Thursday.

That was a morning that changed my life. My gift of encouragement was demonstrated by over twenty people who arrived early that morning. Over the years four or five people would patron the coffee house at any fifteen-minute period, but the shop was packed that day. Each one had signed a card along with special notes. Then one by one, they began to share how I encouraged them over the years. I was blown away. Tears completely drenched my shirt. Without their sharing, I may never had known how God had been using me for that precise purpose. My pastor's words became etched in my heart and mind. Later, I would write a book titled, "The Corner Cafe" to commemorate my emotions of that day.

I realized that my troubled years without parental guidance was used to instill empathy in my heart for others.

1 Corinthians 12 describes several gifts that the Holy Spirit gives to those He pleases. I am sure encouragement was one that I received based on the feedback of that morning. I believe that we endure various setbacks in life for the purpose of using lessons learned for future good. The illustration of buying a new car comes to mind. After driving from the dealership, the same model becomes instantly in our view everywhere we turn. The cars were always there but now it's personal. Experience draws us towards others going through events or situations that we have in our conscious minds. We relate and emphasize with them. I did not remember most of the events that those people in the shop shared, but I related to their words. I could picture being drawn to each situation all over again, despite the many years that passed.

The words of my son came a few years later but served to reinforce the feelings of that day in the coffee house. He was never there, yet he witnessed similar events at other times. I had been encouraging people as part of my normal testimony. One thing to note about spiritual gifts is that the person receiving them rarely knows when they are used to serve others. I must have spoken words of encouragement to others without my knowledge. I have often told people to "Let go and let God." It seemed like a catch phrase but served me well over the years. When I did not know what to say or do, I would internally utter those words to myself. Somehow, the situation in front of me was successfully handled without a conscious effort on my part.

I heard the story of a man who walked the downtown streets of Ft. Lauderdale, Florida every Saturday carrying a sign. It read something like "Seek Jesus. Heaven is Waiting." Those may not have been the exact words but that was his message. Faithfully, he showed up every Saturday to witness for Jesus. The story was shared by a minister preaching at a revival meeting in China, half-way across the world. He shared that a man on the streets of Ft. Lauderdale changed his life. At the end of the conference several men came forward to speak to the minister. They had one thing in common. Namely, they inquired about the man carrying the sign. The minister described him to a tee as the men were awestruck. They also encountered the man in Florida and their lives changed.

The minister and the men agreed to fly to Ft. Lauderdale and try to locate the man with the sign. Although they did not see him, others who knew the man passed on information as to where he could be located. To their dismay, they found him in a hospital bed shrouded by a clear covering maintaining high levels of oxygen. One by one, they shared their testimony and watched tears flow from the man's eyes. Then they saw his lips move as if he was trying to speak. They came closer and heard him say that he had served God every Saturday and this was the first time he ever knew that it had an effect. He passed away that very weekend.

We may not get a sign from God that our purpose was fulfilled in our lifetime like that man. We may not have tears of joy that we accomplished something through faithfulness. God chose to draw near to that man just before his passing as a way of saying "Well done my child." Then He awaited the man with open arms in heaven with exceeding joy. The man left understanding what his purpose on earth was. Many of us still seek the answer to that question.

For me, the corner cafe was more like a steppingstone. God used me to encourage others over a cup of coffee, but He had so much more for me to accomplish. Gifts are given in proportion to our abilities, strengths and other qualities. Some receive many gifts, but believers can rest assured that they will have at least one. My career path took me into the world of electronics. I retired as an electrical engineer. Math and science consumed my educational experience. Reading and writing was at the bottom of my list of skills.

Visiting my dad in Florida after that coffee shop experience defined another purpose for my life. I had no idea how long I would be away from my wife. Dad had a stroke several months before and was confined to a nursing home. His passing created the need for me to share his story. I began writing a memoir which I titled "Legacy of Love." I made spiral bound copies and distributed them to family members and a few friends. I wanted my children to know their grandfather. I was proud of his legacy.

Questions to ponder:

1. Do you understand your purpose in life?

2. Can you examine your life and see where God may have been leading you?

3. What defining moments can you remember?

4. How have they affected you?

RELOCATION

After dad's passing, I continued to work in Florida. My wife made regular trips down for visits, but my travel kept us apart at times. Our daughter was considering moving south so that her husband could find a position with a horticulture company that also provided healthcare. She worked as a special education teacher with benefits and desired to be a stay-at-home mom. When the Atlanta area was chosen for relocation, God's plan for us became known.

My daughter did not know that the training department had considered me to work for them, based on what I had been doing throughout Florida. I had to learn the company's control systems, which required a lot of documentation. As customers needed similar training, I passed my notes on. In addition, I passed the documents to other support personnel across the country including corporate training. The training department was in Atlanta. The department head told me that when a position opened, I would be transferred. That was an answer to prayer as I would limit travel.

I received an email from my daughter letting me know that her husband was interviewing for a position near Atlanta. My heart skipped a beat. I felt that reuniting with my wife and family was part of God's plan. That meant selling two homes and buying one in Georgia. I would reunite with both my wife and daughter. My heart filled with joy as I read her email.

My wife flew down to house hunt for our daughter, her husband, and their children. Little did she know that she would house hunt for us six months later. Selling the home in Florida was quick and I used the equity to purchase the home that my wife selected in Dacula, Georgia, seven miles from where our daughter lived. Home sales in New York took months to close due to legal technicalities. In November 2004, I began teaching in Norcross, Georgia, which was a twenty-five-mile drive towards downtown Atlanta. That was a minimum of forty-five minutes without traffic. Knowing that my wife was near our daughter made the trip bearable.

On the surface, everything felt wonderful. After living in Florida for five years, I was not desiring to fight the winter snow in New York. I also enjoyed playing golf year-round instead of the possible six months. Family was united. Our daughter was homeschooling, and her husband had the benefits they desired. Then the bubble burst.

A few days following Easter 2005, My wife felt a nagging pain in her side. She ignored it for a time thinking that she overate during the celebration. Then she found a doctor who felt a strange mass. The doctor sent her, immediately, to the nearby hospital for a scan. I was conducting a seminar when I received a call. Fear and prayer filled my being as I learned the diagnosis included the dreaded "C" word. A ten-centimeter mass on her liver tested positive as well as other areas on her back and lungs. It was stage four. The back was successfully treated with laser technology. Then three different rounds on chemo were used to treat the other areas. At first, it appeared as though the mass was reducing in size, leaving us hopeful for a cure.

After two years of treatment, the oncologist exhausted every option. The biggest problem was the cancer did not indicate a starting point and was labelled "unknown primary." The final suggestion was an out-of-pocket gene therapy treatment in Houston, Texas. We had applied the money from the sale of the New York house to minimize the loan on the new home but needed to refinance to pay for the new treatments. I made the trip to Houston with my wife, expecting a week or two of gradual treatments. A series of 5mg. pills were initiated to build her up prior to entering the facility. When she built up her body to the level desired by 30mg pills, she would enter the facility.

The first day was not a problem. My wife dropped me off at the nearest coffee shop while she travelled. The next day was harder. She felt tired and we stayed in the motel. After the third day, her signs of pain and weakness were so alarming that we went to have her examined at the facility. They sent her to the nearest hospital where she was diagnosed with pneumonia. The doctors there informed me that they had treated many people from the facility and our hope for a cure was crushed. Only God could save her and that was my prayer. Her vital signs caused me to fly our son down from New York. I thought I would lose her there. My daughter drove in from Georgia.

After they arrived, I received a call from my wife. Her vital signs improved, and she wanted us to bring a dozen donuts to her hospital room. We thought that was strange because she preached the danger of fat grams to us for years. Still, we were excited to satisfy her craving. My daughter asked if she knew where we could find a donut shop. Not only did she share the name and locations, but where the Boston creme donuts were located inside each one. She spent the first day going from donut shop to donut shop while I was at the coffee shop. That was the only way she would know such detail. Then my daughter asked if we should bring some donuts in for the staff. She replied, "You can bring them a dozen, too." We couldn't stop laughing.

Everyone returned home a few days later. I drove separately, while our daughter came back with her mom. My wife seemed to have a time of reprieve and was able to care for herself while I worked. One day my wife and daughter planned to meet me at a bowling alley close to my workplace. I receive a call of urgency and had to leave early. I arrived at the bowling alley where my wife vomited a large amount of blood into a plastic bag. I rushed her to the hospital where she was taken into the ER. I could see her vital signs displayed while outside the room and felt the worst was about to happen. At one point her BP was 20/10. I called her best friend in Florida who was also a retired nurse. We shared and prayed together.

She asked me how I was doing and about my grandchildren. Then she shared something that my wife said that was desperately needed in my life. In an earlier conversation with my wife, the question was raised about how I was handling everything. My wife responded with the words "He's amazing!" She was referring to the fact that she had planned to take the grandchildren out for lunch. Due to illness, she was unable to do that. Without a second thought I took them out. Her words touched something deep within me. I could not remember any time when words of affirmation like that were uttered. I knew that she was always appreciative when did something that helped her or an acquaintance, but a smile or simple "thank you" was all that I heard. It was another defining moment in my life.

The doctors could not locate where the blood came from. Tubes were inserted down her throat and other tests were performed. About midnight she was released from the hospital. We came home, went to bed, and woke suddenly five hours later when the same bloody mess barely made it to the toilet. Somehow, I was able to call 9-1-1. The ambulance arrived quickly, and she was taken to the hospital again. This time they were able to find and repair a cut in the esophagus just above the stomach. Blood had been dripping into the stomach until overflowing. Once again, she was spared and returned home.

The final visit with her oncologist made us aware that we needed to get her affairs in order. My company allowed me to work from home writing training course materials. I was removed from teaching any classes. My wife was gaining weight but with a smile on her face each time she ate a donut. Her best friend flew up to be with her and help relieve some of my stress. I scheduled a meeting with a hospice representative at the hospital and invited my daughter. She made me aware of another hospice worker who lived in our area and was a close friend. I told her to have her meet me at the hospital an hour before my appointment. The rep showed up, introduced herself and handed me her portfolio. I opened it and to my surprise were the words "Legacy of Love."

I handed it to my daughter and said, "Look at that!" In response she replied, "That's your book, dad!" The rep asked if I was a writer. I told her that I had written a book after my dad's passing, had it printed, and gave it to family members. They needed to know that their grandfather or great grandfather was in heaven. I wanted them to know all about him. Another lady in the room overheard our conversation and inserted the words, "You've got to publish that!" I had heard those words many times before. On one occasion I met a writer in a coffee shop who was working on a thousand-page book about the Civil War. After learning about my brief exploits as a writer, he uttered the same words. Then he wrote the name of a book on the back of his business card that helped him get published. I remember thanking him and placed the card in my wallet. The lady continued to share how she received words to write down in the form of hymns and that she did not sing. She read a few and I was impressed.

Because the rep was a friend and lived close by, I signed with her. When the original hospice rep showed up, I let her know that her services would not be needed or so I thought. The next day I learned that I could not use the first hospice due to restrictions on my insurance and made the call to use the second rep. That left me with a lot of questions directed towards God.

Why did this happen?

Why did I meet my daughter's hospice friend and not use her services?

Why did I hear the words of the hymns from that lady?

Then the answer came loud and clear. It was like the

preverbal two-by-four just cracked my skull wide open. I had to publish my book. I thought it was something for my family only and took such a stand, but God had other plans. I began searching for the business card with the book tile. After I found it, I went to the local bookstore, purchased it and then made a feeble attempt to follow through with its instructions. It may have been helpful for the man I met in the coffee shop but was confusing for me. I did some research but could not escape the fact that there was something more. Then I turned the card over and everything started to make sense.

The card had the man's name, business and other information, but the words "Houston, Texas" leaped out. I thought I was going there to help my wife, but God wanted me to meet that man. I was only in that coffee shop the first day. Everything escalated after that. I had a new purpose. God desired my dad's story to reach the world. I started searching various Christian publishing agents and landed on Tate Publishing. I added my wife's story to the original work and published "Legacy of Love" in 2008. My wife died on June 1, 2007, and her legacy needed to be preserved as well.

God was not through. The first book given to nonfamily members went to a coworker. My wife's passing came on the same day as my second retirement. I felt some guilt working from home during the month of May and decided to spend the last days in hospice with my wife. Soon afterwards, the company hired me as a consultant to write course materials and conduct training classes. The materials that I worked on in May turned out to be a huge revenue source of training for the company and I was the only one able to teach it. I also had to train the trainers. That involved a lot of travelling, which also helped me escape the loneliness of an empty house.

I arrived at the Norcross office to pick up materials for a class when Katie met me. Katie was an Afro-American lady that I trained and knew for about eight years. To my knowledge she was unmarried but had a hyphenated last name. I gave her the book, picked up my supplies and left. Two weeks later, I returned to pick up materials for a new class, when Katie leaped up and hugged me. She said, "I read your book." I told her that I hoped she enjoyed it, and she responded, "You don't understand. I gave it to my ex-husband to read." Again, I shared that I hoped he enjoyed it as well. "You still don't understand." Then she held up her left hand with a light from a wedding band nearly blinding me. They remarried.

I don't know what they read that rejoined their hearts. Much of the book is described from the heart of the child in me that was abandoned. Perhaps, they related to those emotional scars. Whatever the reason, they remarried after they both read the book. God knew that would happen. He knew that the book was not just for family members. To Him we are part of a bigger family. I wondered if my stubbornness to publish led to my wife's demise. Perhaps, her story needed to be included to complete the couple's reunion. Many thoughts began to enter my mind, but one thing was certain. God knew the whole picture. I was His messenger.

Questions to ponder:

1. Have you had a time of separation from family in your life?

2. If so, what did you learn from the experience?

3. Have you ever found yourself outside your comfort zone?

4. If so, how did you handle it?

KNOWING OUR PURPOSE

riting became therapy for me after my wife's passing. Except for writing my dad's story, I didn't see myself as a writer. I was an electrical engineer. I loved to use my hands making things. Hitting keystrokes was a far cry from woodworking. Still, I migrated from writing textbooks and manuals to short stories. Typing is still a hunt and peck exercise. The silence of an empty house is deafening. I needed something to take my mind off my grief and heal at the same time.

June 1 is a date that is far more than a memorial. It is our daughter's wedding anniversary and their daughter, Kelly's birthday. I still remember my daughter saying, "Why did mom have to leave on this day?" Kelly was born with a heart defect and when she got older would need an operation. The last time my wife was in the hospital, Kelly was in another one several miles away. I was torn between being with my wife and seeing my granddaughter. Her operation was successful, and relief came quickly.

Kelly had a special bond with her grammy. When "Grammy" died, her grief lingered. She would sit next to me in church and cry. I decided to help her overcome that grief.

My wife had purchased two AAA books that were used to record life events to be passed on after our passing. I found them but had a difficult time answering the questions, especially where they related to her family tree. I decided to put a book together that covered many of the same things but with events that I was knowledgeable about. I gathered thousands of photos as far back as I could and created an eighty-page spiral bound book titled:

Things Grammy wants Bryce and Kelly to know.

October 12, 1944 – June 1, 2007

Each page was filled with a "Did you know ..." line followed by a picture. For example, I wrote "Did you know Grammy looked like this as a child." followed by her baby picture.

Did you know Grammy looked like this as a child?

"Did you know that this was my first car " followed by a picture of her car. There were over a hundred of "Did you know" lines until the final page. There I placed her picture with the words, "Now you know."

Other versions of the book were created for my son, daughter, brothers, etc. Those had to be modified because she was not "Grammy" to them. References to my son would have been their uncle. My father would have been their grandfather. The books had to be personalized if they could help overcome grief.

Then I decided to write a book geared for a five-year old to understand. She could understand pictures as reminders and learn about things unfamiliar to her. But I had a desire to help her understand that "Grammy" was in a place called heaven and that someday Kelly would see her again. I put together a stapled 5.5" x 8.5" booklet titled, "The Acorn and the Oak tree." I told a story of an oak tree (grammy) going through the seasons of the year, hoping to see an acorn (Kelly) fall to the ground, sprout, and begin to grow into a tree. Her father worked in horticulture and trained his children in his field. He handed them various acorns, pecans, walnuts, etc. and then showed them the tree that produced them. I hoped this story would hit home.

In the story, squirrels would gather the acorns dashing the oak tree's hopes until one day an acorn sprouted, and a smile could be seen on the tree's trunk. After passing several seasons with the new tree showing growth, the oak tree dies, leaving only a leafless skeleton. A new golden leaf tree appears (heaven) with joy watching the little tree grow. In the end, the golden leaf tree is seen with Grammy's picture. She is seen leaping with arms spread while smiling.

I gave Kelly that book for Christmas and her grief turned to healing shortly after. Then she asked me to write a new book for next Christmas. She didn't tell me what it would be about, only that it had to come from "Papa."

Because Kelly was heavy into animals, I chose three animals from the other side of the earth. I wanted it to have a similar theme and a lesson to keep her seeking God. I titled the book "The Koala, the Wombat and the Dingo." The same stapled 5.5" x 8.5" format was used. As I write this Kelly is twenty-two, working with animals as a veterinary technician and working on a degree in her field. Both books have been re-illustrated and published within the last three years. The "Acorn and the Oak Tree" leaves a placeholder on the last page for a loved one's picture, so that it can apply to anyone going through grief.

Questions to ponder:

1. Do you know your purpose in life?

2. How do you define it?

3. What do you believe is the reason for it?

4. What evidence do you see or feel that encourages pursuing it?

FULFILLING OUR PURPOSE

Writing as therapy is only as good as how well the works complete our healing. That part tends to be attached to how well the writing affects others. Does it provide meaning or encouragement? When I read what I penned the next day, does it illuminate or appear as nonsense? I began recalling people and events that had an impact on my life. These started as short stories that had their origin far in my past. The first one was titled, "Molly's Story."

As a devoted husband, I am not in the habit of engaging women outside my home, family or friends. Molly came into the coffee shop one morning with an intense sadness or aura about her. She ordered a cup of tea, sat down on the stool next to me and hung her head. I felt that she was troubled, tapped her on the shoulder and introduced myself.

"Excuse me ma'am. You don't know me. My name is Dennis. I sense something is wrong in your life. Can I help you?"

Molly responded without hesitation. It was as if she wanted someone or something to help her through a crisis. My introduction caused her to unleash a barrage of events in her life. Her husband was going blind. He couldn't drive so she had to take him to work. He was about to receive a medical retirement that meant a great reduction in income. She was a stay-at-home mom without a resume. She would need to find work to offset the loss in revenue. One son was applying to college. The other was a year behind. She was probably ten to fifteen years older than I, based on the age of her sons. My oldest child was not yet a teenager.

Before I could catch my breath from the onslaught, I was led to share a story about my dad. I told her that my mom died when I was three and he remarried when I was eight. My new mom was instrumental in raising three boys and helping dad get on his feet. Later they retired and moved to Florida where she began to lose her eyesight. Then I said something like, "But Molly, dad never looked at it like you." Those words caused her to lift her head as she asked, "How did your dad handle it?" I continued sharing that my father counted it a blessing as he recalled all that she had done for him. Now he was able to give back. Helping her bathe and cooking a meal became acts of joy and love.

I remember watching scales fall from her eyes. The story must have been placed on my lips for me to share as I felt the words came from somewhere well outside my mind. Perhaps, the fact that it was based on my observation of my father during mom's final years. I remember sitting on her bed in their apartment, when dad began to talk about all the things that he had to do for her in her final days. Then he said words like, "if she wants to come back, she is welcome." Those words spoke volumes. All I know is that the words left my mouth before any thought. Molly thanked me and I asked if I could pray for her before leaving for work. She agreed.

I never knew her last name but saw her in the coffee shop for the next seventeen years. I saw her get a job in the hospital about five minutes away. She worked the night shift and got off at six AM. Usually, she entered the coffee shop within minutes after I arrived. In other words, she did not go straight home after work. I saw her sons' graduation and wedding pictures as the years passed. She also became a grandmother. Her husband's eyesight did not lead to total blindness as they still enjoyed trips together sharing the various sights. Life seemed good as she always greeted me with a smile and often a hug.

So why did this story have such a profound effect on me as I began writing her story? The answer came when I left for Florida after retiring as I shared earlier. On normal days the shop held four of five people in any fifteen-minute timeframe. This was not a normal day. The coffee shop was filled with people. One by one they approached me and shared how I had encouraged them over the years. Molly was the last one to share.

"Remember when you met me?"

"Sure, your husband was going blind...medical retirement... stay-at-home mom..."

"You don't know the rest of the story!"

Tears had already drenched my clothes from the words shared by all the others. More started flowing as I anxiously waited for her to continue.

"That day, I had an appointment with my doctor. I was under his care for severe depression. When I walked into his office he said these words to me, 'Molly! What happened to you?' Those words frightened me. I asked him 'Why do you ask?'"

The doctor said, "You look so upbeat today."

"I just met this wonderful man in a coffee shop. Then I shared the story of your father with him."

"Do you know what he said to me?"

Crying, I replied, "I hope you're going to tell me."

"He said, 'Molly, you don't need me anymore. Just keep going to that coffee shop.'"

WOW! What an impact those words had on me. I just went though so many acts of encouragement from the other patrons. Not only was I used to encourage Molly, but she just put an exclamation mark on how God had used me during the everyday interactions with people that I would only contact at that place. It also explained why Molly never went directly home after working all night at the hospital. I was fulfilling the doctor's prescription for her. I understood why I didn't break the habit of visiting the coffee shop after retiring. God had me right where he wanted and provided undeniable affirmation that I was being used by Him. It was a defining moment. No wonder why it popped into my head as the first story that I wrote in my therapy session after my wife died.

Other people that came into my life involving coffee began resurfacing. I wrote ten or twelve stories and spiral bound them. As people read them, I was told that I should have titled the book, "Divine Appointments." That idea took hold. I began to write other stories that placed me in the right place at the right time. With each one, I felt god's purpose for my life was being fulfilled. Helping my father return to the Lord was only a start of my life's purpose. Writing began as therapy but turned into a way to use the gift of encouragement.

Remember Katie, the woman who remarried after reading my first published book? She sent the spiral bound coffee shop book to her Godmother in South Florida. Her name was Isileen Webb. She was a Baptist pastor who lost her husband eight years earlier. She read the stories and called Katie.

"Where has this man been?"

Katie shared with me later what those words meant. Isileen was still in mourning over the loss of her husband. Time had not healed her. Somehow, the words she read brought comfort and closure to her heart and soul. I believe that God knew that beforehand. He may have used my fingers to tap the very keys that would penetrate her heart. Isileen went on to share another incident with Katie. She was on her way to church one Sunday and suddenly turned around and drove home. She left the "Coffee Shop Ministries" book on the kitchen counter. It was like a child's blanket that helped them sleep. It went everywhere with her.

After listening to Katie share, I asked if it would be all right if I wrote Isileen's story as evidence of a divine appointment. She not only agreed but Isileen desired to write a review. I titled her story "The Pastor." She wrote these words:

> *Thank you for your gift of sharing God's love through your writings...especially for allowing me to sip tea at your "Coffee Shop Cafe". Just reading about the encounters added light to many dismal days. Oh, how I long for your coffee shop fellowship during these times." Isileen Webb (Florida)*

Knowing that those stories had such an effect on someone that I never met, especially a pastor, let me know that my purpose was being fulfilled. More memories of divine appointments began to surface. A Florida friend began placing one story each month on their website. After the first month they noticed viewers logged in the following month at a high rate. Hits quadrupled. My friend's son was an accomplished golfer. I rented a cart to watch him play a high school match, along with his parents. At one point his parents fell behind. Then they caught up and gave me a name with a phone number to call. The person called them after reading "Molly's Story" on their website. I was instructed to return the call.

After the match I made the call. They were a retired couple living in South Georgia. The husband had been looking for a part time job to offset his low retirement income. They rarely left their home, except for necessities. The idea of meeting people in a coffee shop seemed foreign. I called and introduced myself as the writer of "Molly's Story." They shared how the story touched them along with where they were in life. I remember asking if their town had the "Golden Arches" sign and they affirmed that it did. Along with recommending that they find a church where they could meet people, I suggested that they visit the arches one morning, sip a cup of coffee, and observe people. They kept in touch with me, followed through on suggestions and their lives began to change for the better. Their story was added as another divine appointment and titled "The Seniors." In a short time, the book covered two dozen separate stories. Years later the book was officially published, originally in 2019 by URLink. In order to use one publisher for all my works, it was republished along with "Legacy of Love," which was no longer available. The Christian publisher went out of business.

In 2010 my Florida friend invited me down to interview Jake (not his real name). Jake was a Christian friend with a story to tell. My friend wanted me to write it. I came down and was handed a tape recorder with several tapes to capture the interview. Jake's story became my first novel titled "Shackled Yet Free," published in 2011 with IUniverse. I wanted Jake and my friend to have a means to acquire copies for distribution to their families. Some members of my church also were given copies. After they read it, I was told that they couldn't wait for the next one. That seemed strange, since I thought Jake's words ended in a completed work. Two ladies wanted to know what happened to an illegitimate son fathered by Jake when he was far from the Lord. Jake had an affair with a married woman, whose husband was fighting a war in Iraq. She got pregnant and Jake bolted. I found myself writing a sequel based on what those ladies desired.

The first novel was based on a true story. Only the ending was fictionalized. The second one had to be all fiction, testing my writing skills to the limit. Somehow, I began with a simple thought. Jake would meet his full-grown son as part of God's plan for his changed life. Each night I put my thoughts on paper. Each morning, I would read the section from the night before with amazement. It was as if someone else was hitting the keys. That continued for about two weeks when the work was finished. I titled it "Freedom's Journey." I printed a copy for the ladies to read and gave it to them.

Then I opened my computer to consider a third book as a trilogy. I thought about a father-son newfound relationship and how that would transpire. The result was titled "Free to

Serve." To save publishing costs, both books were published as one publication by IUniverse the following year. Again, I republished all three books separately with my current publisher. That process came ten years later after I received high marks from professional readers. I knew there were some grammatical errors and reread each book to make the corrections. As I reviewed the second and third books in the trilogy, I found myself in amazement. I knew that I hit the keystrokes, but I did not remember where I was going with the plots. Once again, it was as if someone else wrote it.

I believe that God provided the words as I entered them on the paper. If that was the case, then they were placed there for a purpose. Time will tell what that purpose was. All I knew for sure was that I could write novels. That was a far cry from short stories or children's books. I was now a writer with many genres. By the way. Those ladies also enjoyed the sequels.

Short stories, children's books and novels seemed like a natural progression in the learning process for a new writer. Still, there was more to do. I do not believe in things happening by accident. From an engineer mentality, writing appeared so foreign to problem solving and applying logic. My time spent away from work was better served doing crosswords or logic problems, than reading. Even during those times, my mind would work overtime trying to solve a work-related problem. Writing made no sense until the loss of my wife and grief entered in. Losing her was not logical. I tried to find logical answers. I lost her acts of love, but God began a work of love in me.

Ephesians 2:10 assured me that I was loved before I was even born. All my experiences had a purpose and now everything began to make sense. My wife was God's gift to help me overcome the loss of love during my childhood. We are not on this earth by accident. God is love and desires to share that with His creation. He does not wish that anyone should perish (John3:16, Matt.18:14). I know that my wife is in His loving arms, and I will join her someday. But, God has more for me to do and writing is part of the process.

Questions to ponder:

1. What do you feel are your qualifications to fulfill your purpose?

2. What caused you to recognize your purpose?

3. Where are you headed as you fulfill your purpose?

4. What confirmation have you received?

NEW DIRECTION

The newest direction in my life involves writing true life stories for others, much like my first novel nearly twenty years earlier. Jake's story did not have an ending as he shared several areas still left unfinished. I was forced to fictionalize an ending to make his story complete for readers. It wasn't until the spring of 2024 that I was approached to write another true-life story. This one had an ending that occurred in 2016, eight years earlier. Kent and Sandye (actual names) were the lead characters. Around 2017 a neighbor heard their story and began making audio tapes for the purpose of finding someone to write it. The timing, especially for Sandye, was not right.

There is no doubt that God preselected and prepared me for that task. Kent's neighbor started attending my church but didn't meet me until he attended a Tuesday morning Bible study / breakfast at a local restaurant. After someone shared that I was a writer, an instant bond took place. I was the answer to his prayers. Initially, I began writing a third person account based on the tapes that I received. But things got very jumbled. Kent was a great storyteller but skipped around far too much. I needed to stop and contact Kent directly. That resulted in a collaboration as hebegan to retell his story in the first person. "Joy Through the Journey" became available early in 2025. Hundreds of lives have been affected already as Kent has testified in front of coworkers, churches and friends. I joined him one day in Alabama, where he was invited to speak in front of two hundred food service workers. Each participant received a copy of the book as he used the money received to purchase them. many of them provided five-star ratings on Amazon as they were deeply moved.

Others have approached me to write their stories as well. It seems that many people have testimonies that can lead people to Jesus, but without the skills to get them in print. A sequel to Kent's story is also being considered. I find it true joy to listen to others share testimonies. My heart is touched as theirs is revealed. Retirement is not waiting for God to take me. It is allowing Him to use me to help others before my time on earth is over. I look forward to what He has for me next to both learn and accomplish.

Questions to ponder:

1. What are the roads in life that you have travelled?

2. What did you learn along each path?

3. Where do you think you will head next?

4. Are you where God wants you?

FINISH THE RACE

*K*nowing that God has a plan for my life is rewarding. The words "That's just like you, dad" could lead to words like "That's just like Jesus." What a powerful thought. Yet, the more we follow God's plan for our lives, the more they begin to ring true. Paul was a Pharisee with a zeal to protect Jewish laws and customs that he believed were true. After his encounter with Jesus, everything changed. Philippians 1:21 is Paul's words after his conversion.

"For to me, to live is Christ and to die is gain."

Paul knew that whatever work he was called to do was intended to draw people to Christ. If he died, then he would be with Christ for eternity. He faced shipwrecks, beatings, prison and other hardships but counted it all joy. Listen to some of his words.

Philippians 3:1-10:

> [7] *But whatever were gains to me I now consider loss for the sake of Christ.* [8] *What is more, I consider everything a loss because of the surpassing worth of knowing Christ Jesus my Lord, for whose sake I have lost all things. I consider them garbage, that I may gain Christ* [9] *and be found in him, not having a righteousness of my own that comes from the law, but that which is through faith in*[a] *Christ— the righteousness that comes from God on the basis of faith.* [10] *I want to know Christ—yes, to know the power of his resurrection and participation in his sufferings, becoming like him in his death,*

Acts 20:22-25:

> [22] *"And now, compelled by the Spirit, I am going to Jerusalem, not knowing what will happen to me there.* [23] *I only know that in every city the Holy Spirit warns me that prison and hardships are facing me.* [24] *However, I consider my life worth nothing to me; my only aim is to finish the race and complete the task the Lord Jesus has given me—the task of testifying to the good news of God's grace.*

Acts 16:25-30:

> [25] *About midnight Paul and Silas were praying and singing hymns to God, and the other prisoners were listening to them.* [26] *Suddenly there was such a violent earthquake that the foundations of the*

prison were shaken. At once all the prison doors flew open, and everyone's chains came loose. ²⁷ The jailer woke up, and when he saw the prison doors open, he drew his sword and was about to kill himself because he thought the prisoners had escaped. ²⁸ But Paul shouted, "Don't harm yourself! We are all here!"

²⁹ The jailer called for lights, rushed in and fell trembling before Paul and Silas.³⁰ He then brought them out and asked, "Sirs, what must I do to be saved?"

Even after his chains were broken and the prison doors opened, Paul knew his purpose was not to escape, but to show Jesus to the man guarding him. Then we read the unity between Paul and his friend Silas as they completed God's purpose for them.

Acts 16:31-35:

³¹ They replied, "Believe in the Lord Jesus, and you will be saved—you and your household." ³² Then they spoke the word of the Lord to him and to all the others in his house. ³³ At that hour of the night the jailer took them and washed their wounds; then immediately he and all his household were baptized. ³⁴ The jailer brought them into his house and set a meal before them; he was filled with joy because he had come to believe in God—he and his whole household.

The jailor would have killed himself for fear of reprisal from the Romans for allowing prisoners to escape, yet Paul shouted (vs.28) for him to stop. Then the guard and his whole family were saved for a heavenly reunion with Jesus.

Like Paul, we have been called to lead others to Christ. That may not be as dramatic as this account in Paul's writing. Paul spoke about finishing the race. He knew his calling and desired to complete it strong. His reward would be the words "Well done my child" from the lips of his Savior. My wife finished her race and left this earth with a peaceful spirit. Her work was done, while mine only just began. It has been nearly nineteen years since her passing, and I am in a marathon.

Questions to ponder:

1. How are you finishing the race?

2. Have you ever felt like stopping?

3. Do you feel that you are in a sprint or marathon?

4. What obstacles impede you?

SUPPORT SYSTEM

*I*f there is one thing that life has taught me, it's that we are not meant to navigate through alone. God said from the very beginning that "it is not good for the man to be alone" (Genesis 2:18) and created a helpmate for Adam. Prior to Eve entering Adam's life, God was his support. Imagine a conversation between them as Adam tried to make sense of all that was happening. Adam had questions. God provided answers. Each answer might lead to more questions and so on. Adam was created for communion with his creator. For God, that part was "very good." Adam had the breath of God inside but was not designed as God's alter ego or puppet. God loved his creation and desired for that love to be returned. That same scenario should be instilled in earthly fathers. With Eve as his helpmate, that process could be fulfilled.

God also desired more and commanded his creation to multiply and fill the earth. Men and women were to unite as one flesh to nurture offspring in one accord. The support parents receive from their parents prepared them to be the necessary support for their children. Straying from God's plan involved parental separation. From the very beginning we are told about Adam and Eve's disobedience. Eve was swayed by a serpent and ate the fruit. Then Adam followed by listening to Eve. They were expelled from God's presence and began multiplying the earth. Their disobedience (sin) caused Cain to kill his brother. The source of parental support broke down as Cain wandered.

The concept of support is further illustrated in the building of a house. It will not withstand the onslaught of nature's elements like heavy winds and torrential downpours. Sandcastles made from sand on a beach will quickly erode and fall when the ocean's high tide comes in. For anything to last, the foundation must be considered first. It must be on solid ground and deep enough to support the weight. Living in upstate New York taught me that when winter comes, the ground freezes. Underground wiring and water lines need to be at least three feet below the surface so when the ground freezes, its expansion does not cause them to break. If builders tried to cut corners, there would be a rude awakening someday. Cracked cement comes from the house settling, because the foundation was not on solid ground. The same can be seen when sinkholes appear on roads that were the underlying support was inadequate.

The question of where we get our support is a good one. If we examine our lives, we may see that it comes more from friends, coworkers, or the internet than from our parents. Time spent on cell phones or various media may be consuming us. When parents are viewed as providers only, the support system breaks down. It is no wonder why school shootings, gang violence and other needless events have become more and more prevalent as divorce and single parent homes are on the rise. Two family incomes may add to the problem as children are left alone or without strong support. Children learn from their environment or lack of it. So, what is the answer?

Jesus speaks to that very clearly in Matthew after addressing a large crowd on the hillside. His words have been referred to as "the Sermon on the Mount," starting with chapter five. Then in chapter seven we read these words:

> 24 *"Therefore, everyone who hears these words of mine and puts them into practice is like a wise man who built his house on the rock.* 25 *The rain came down, the streams rose, and the winds blew and beat against that house; yet it did not fall, because it had its foundation on the rock.* 26 *But everyone who hears these words of mine and does not put them into practice is like a foolish man who built his house on sand.* 27 *The rain came down, the streams rose, and the winds blew and beat against that house, and it fell with a great crash."*

> 28 *When Jesus had finished saying these things, the crowds were amazed at his teaching,*

> 29 *because he taught as one who had authority, and not as their teachers of the law.*

Verses 28 - 29 added emphasis. Jesus did not teach like the Jewish leaders. He taught with authority. Those who listened to His words were amazed. I look back at my life with the same amazement. I felt inadequate as a father until God took the reins. My son's affirmation was one sign. Those words in that coffee shop was another that He was in control. The support that I received may have come through others, but I am certain that God was directing it. When unexplained things happen, I often joke about them as coincidences. Then I chuckle as I don't believe in chance. Dad did not survive three days alone in his apartment, nor did he come back to Jesus by chance. It was no coincidence that I have been called to write as well. My support system may have started with parental guidance, but God took the wheel.

Questions to ponder:

1. Where do you get your support?

2. What does your support system look like?

3. What have you learned?

4. How important is having support?

OBJECT LESSONS

One of the best ways to train a child comes from using observational techniques that bring the lesson home. Jesus used several parables for this purpose. When words are replaced with pictures, our memory improves. When my son returned home after four years of college, he needed one of those lessons. He still lacked courses for completion, but our financial support was now focused on our daughter. He knew that he needed to find employment but did not have a vehicle. My car had a blue book value of forty-five-hundred dollars and would serve his needs, but he needed to secure a loan. The five-hundred-dollar limit on a credit card that was issued to him when he entered college had a balance of eight-hundred-dollars due to minimum or missed payments. The great deal that he got on stereo speakers four years earlier did not seem as good then.

I told him that I would sell him my car for three-thousand, and he was to secure a loan for thirty-eight hundred. That sounded like a good plan. The blue book value alone should provide collateral. After a long time, he returned with the words "I couldn't get a loan, dad." I think he was startled when I said, "I knew that." Then I told him to get in the car, and we would go get the loan. In an angry voice re responded, "Didn't you hear me? I couldn't get a loan!" I told him that I heard him. Then I said that I could cosign as collateral and off we went. The loan was secured under my name. Two bank checks were issued. One went in my pocket to cover the car cost, while the other was sent to pay off his credit card.

After living at home for several months, he decided to find a place on his own. He seemed to be drawn to computer systems and was faithful making his loan payments. Shortly after moving out, I received a phone call.

"Dad. You'll never guess what I just purchased."

"A computer, printer, and other system needs."

"How did you know that?"

"That was all you talked about when you were home."

"You are right, but that's not the best part. I went to the bank and secured a loan on my signature."

He paid off the car loan early and established a good credit report. He has managed money well ever since. It was a lesson well learned. i was pleased as my credit took a hit by cosigning and that was gone. I hope that he received a strong thumbs up from me at the time. Later, he secured a well-paying job in the software industry as well.

The object lessons are intended to obtain desired results in a short time. Often, they become personal in nature. One father, during a morning men's Bible study, shared a lesson used with his son the night before. He began speaking about his son's misbehavior. He told his son to go to the place where punishment was issued in the past. His son obeyed. After a reasonable amount of time had passed, designed for his son to think about what he had done, dad entered carrying the usual instrument used for punishment. He then asked his son if he understood what he did. His son was remorseful and nodded that he understood. Then his father made the lesson unforgettable. He handed his son the instrument to hold while he knelt in front in front of his son with the following words:

> *"I want you to strike me. You realize that you did wrong, but I desire to take your punishment."*

> *"No, dad. I can't do that."*

> *"You must. strike me hard."*

After a little more dialog, with tears in his eyes, he swung the rod.

"Harder son." The blow was applied.

"Again, son. Again."

With each blow, dad could feel the pain as well as his son's sadness. Then the lesson was complete as dad hugged his son and shared how Jesus took our punishment, though we deserved it. Many parents utter these words prior to administering punishment, "This is going to hurt me more than it does you." Those words do not make sense to the child about to receive the rod. This dad made it become real. It was a lesson well learned. The son carried it with him for life.

Jesus demonstrated an object lesson in John, chapter eight. The religious leaders brought a woman caught in adultery before Jesus with the intent to trap him. Punishment for her offense by law was stoning. Jesus was preaching love and forgiveness. Either Jesus would challenge the law and not have her stoned, or He would have her stoned, negating His message of forgiveness. These are John's words:

> *²At dawn he appeared again in the temple courts, where all the people gathered around him, and he sat down to teach them. ³ The teachers of the law and the Pharisees brought in a woman caught in adultery. They made her stand before the group ⁴ and said to Jesus, "Teacher, this woman was caught in the act of adultery. ⁵ In the Law Moses commanded us to stone such women. Now what do you say?" ⁶ They were using this question as a trap, in order to have a basis for accusing him.*

> *But Jesus bent down and started to write on the ground with his finger. ⁷ When they kept on questioning him, he straightened up and said to them, "Let any one of you who is without sin be the first to throw a stone at her." ⁸ Again he stooped down and wrote on the ground.*

> *⁹ At this, those who heard began to go away one at a time, the older ones first, until only Jesus was left, with the woman still standing there. ¹⁰ Jesus straightened up and asked her, "Woman, where are they? Has no one condemned you?"*

> *¹¹ "No one, sir," she said.*

> *"Then neither do I condemn you," Jesus declared. "Go now and leave your life of sin."*

Notice how Jesus responded in verse six and again in verse eight. He bent down and wrote in the ground. He did not answer immediately. We can only guess what he wrote. That was not the issue. Those holding the stones had to pause. Verse seven provides His answer. He supported the law and punishment but challenged all who were ready to carry out the punishment to ponder their own lives. No one could say they were without sin, and they left. Love won, leaving the Jewish leaders with mud on their faces. The lesson was designed to obtain mercy. Oh God, that's just like you. Jesus puts an exclamation point on it in verse eleven as He offers his forgiveness to the woman. Many Bible scholars believe that she repented and became a follower.

On a humorous note, I recalled a time when I used an object lesson as an ice breaker following a break for lunch. Ice breakers are designed to improve the student attentiveness following a lunch break. One student, I will call Joe, did not seem to take notes and I was concerned, Before the class started that morning, I spoke to two class members who came with Joe from the same company. They assure me that Joe was "getting it." Joe had two master's degrees and had a photographic memory. I started that afternoon with a question.

"Does anyone know why Bill Gates dropped out of college and started Microsoft?"

Although my answer was a play on words, Joe seemed to perk up. It was as if the question was close to his heart. Perhaps his goal was to retire young as a multi-millionaire. I began by telling them that Bill was taking a science class when he learned the definition of the word "power." I then proceeded to write the following formula on the white board:

POWER = WORK / TIME.

Then I made the following substitutions, based on alternative synonyms for power and time using knowledge and money:

KNOWLEDGE = WORK / MONEY

I transposed the equation to read:

MONEY = WORK / KNOWLEDGE

Since Bill desired to make money, Bill dropped out of school because he realized that the more he learned, the less he would earn. Joe blurted out a four-letter word and hung his head. The class groaned and laughed almost in unison. They groaned, because they realized that the ice breaker was just a play on words, except for Joe. They broke out in laughter after they heard Joe's cry. At any rate, the class was alert for that afternoon. I could only imagine what was going through Joe's mind. With two master's degrees, he must have spent many years attending college classes. Did he believe the lesson as truth and not just a game of word play? When the class ended and Joe left the room, Joe's coworkers confronted me.

"You really nailed Joe."

"I guess you were right telling me that he was "getting it."

"He got it alright."

I only wished that my son was in the class that day as he would have said, "that's just like you, dad." Whenever we are together, I tend to make light of mundane things, resulting in a burst of laughter and a bantering between us. It is something that we look forward to, whenever we get together. Sometimes, that happens over a phone conversation as well.

Often, we are taught using words alone. Rarely, do they take root. Applications and examples tend to involve all our senses. Object lessons can make the training come alive like seeds planted on fertile soil.

Questions to ponder:

1. What object lessons have you used to change someone's direction?

2. What lessons have been used by others to change your behavior?

3. How long have the effects lasted?

4. Have you ever applied a lesson learned to help another?

NEW CHALLENGES

*A*s long as we have breath, God can use us. As I share my life stories with others, I become acquainted with new ones. Many people say words like "I need to write my story" or "I wish I could put my life into words like you." It is as though God wants to use me to help others leave their legacy.

I stated that I do not believe in things happening by chance. This year has been filled with highs and lows in my life. Soon after I completed "Joy Through the Journey," I was diagnosed with prostate cancer. After five weeks of radiation treatments and hormone therapy, my urologist told me that things look good that the cancer was gone. I must continue the hormone pills for at least another year, which leaves me easily fatigued. I can still play golf but must limit any extra exertion. Writing does not have any adverse effect. In fact, I joke about using it as a weight reduction program. I find myself writing for hours, thus skipping meals without feeling the hunger pains.

The combination of hearing inspiring stories from others and serving God through writing becomes a new challenge. Kent desires to write a sequel about how God continues to lead him over the past nine years since his book ended. Another friend of his started communication with me for his life story, until cancer returned in his wife. Perhaps, that story will be completed with a new ending. Sorting through so many true-life stories requires God's leading as to which one needs to be my next work. Still, I feel a high level of joy and excitement knowing that He has something for me to do that will bring glory to Him and others to heaven's gates.

Perhaps, God has other plans like public speaking or film media. Over the past three years I have been bombarded by various literary agents, motion film producers and publishing houses intent of promoting several of my previous works. Several of these seemed so real that I felt they must be part of God's leading. After taking a financial loss, I learned that was not the case. Now, when I am approached, red flags go up. If something offered is truly real, then God will speak volumes. Financial outlay on my part is an instant refusal to any offer. My challenge is waiting on Him.

Jesus uttered the words "It is finished" just before taking His last breath while nailed to a wooden cross. His disciples may have understood what those words meant after hearing Jesus share these words in Matthew 16:21-27:

> 21 *From that time on Jesus began to explain to his disciples that he must go to Jerusalem and suffer many things at the hands of the elders, the chief priests and the teachers of the law, and that he must be killed and on the third day be raised to life.*

²² Peter took him aside and began to rebuke him. "Never, Lord!" he said. "This shall never happen to you!"

²³ Jesus turned and said to Peter, "Get behind me, Satan! You are a stumbling block to me; you do not have in mind the concerns of God, but merely human concerns."

²⁴ Then Jesus said to his disciples, "Whoever wants to be my disciple must deny themselves and take up their cross and follow me. ²⁵ For whoever wants to save their life will lose it, but whoever loses their life for me will find it.²⁶ What good will it be for someone to gain the whole world, yet forfeit their soul? Or what can anyone give in exchange for their soul? ²⁷ For the Son of Man is going to come in his Father's glory with his angels, and then he will reward each person according to what they have done.

He told His disciples that the Jewish leaders were going to take Him to be killed. Then He told them in verse twenty-four to "take up their cross" and follow Him. They may have witnessed crucifixion by the Romans to understand what that meant. The scene of Jesus hanging on one would make those words come alive. Jesus made it even more personal as He told them to take up their own cross if they wanted to be His disciples. Following Him would cost them everything but eternal life was held in the balance. Jesus died so that we might live with him in eternity. Our life here on earth is only a blink of an eye in comparison. We must use it wisely.

What a joy it is to know that God uses everyday people

like me to continue His work until he comes again, which he promises in verse twenty-seven. When that happens, rewards will be issued to faithful servants. How sad it will be for those who place their trust in worldly things and lose their soul. "Joy Through the Journey" may have been the title of Kent and Sandye's life but it also can be used for everyone following Jesus.

Questions to ponder:

1. Where do you think God will lead you next?

2. What do you think you will be doing?

3. Do you believe that you will be equipped?

4. What do you think your legacy will be?

CONCLUSION

"That's just like you."

- What words describe your life?
- What do others see in you?
- What areas of your life do you feel remorse or wish you could change?
- Can you look back and see how your life's ambitions changed your course?
- Have you accepted Christ in your heart?
- Are you following Him and is He leading you?
- Have you encouraged others who touched your life?
- Do you have joy in your heart that only comes from knowing Jesus?
- Have you found purpose for your life?
- Are you fulfilling the purpose God has for you?
- Do you understand why you endured pain or hardships in the past?

These and many more questions may have entered your mind as you read this work. Just as my son's words had a profound effect on me, it is my hope that you are leaving a legacy of love, joy, and hope representing the life you have lived. If not, then I pray that your life changes so that others receive these qualities. God is in the business of changed lives. May God bless you.

www.ingramcontent.com/pod-product-compliance
Lightning Source LLC
Chambersburg PA
CBHW020327130626
46549CB00003B/1059